The Collection of the Museum at FIT

Fashion Designers A–Z

TASCHEN

December / January

Monday **30**
Montag
Lundi
Lunes

Tuesday **31**
Dienstag
Mardi
Martes

(USA) (UK) (D) (F) (E)
New Year's Day | Neujahr |
Jour de l'An | Año Nuevo

● **1**
Wednesday
Mittwoch
Mercredi
Miércoles

(UK) *Public Holiday (Scotland only)*

Thursday **2**
Donnerstag
Jeudi
Jueves

Friday **3**
Freitag
Vendredi
Viernes

Saturday **4**
Samstag
Samedi
Sábado

Sunday **5**
Sonntag
Dimanche
Domingo

January

Week 2 *Januar Janvier Enero*

6

Monday

Montag
Lundi
Lunes

Ⓓ Ⓔ *Heilige Drei Könige (teilw.) | Reyes*

7

Tuesday

Dienstag
Mardi
Martes

---

8   ◖

Wednesday

Mittwoch
Mercredi
Miércoles

9

Thursday

Donnerstag
Jeudi
Jueves

IO

Friday

Freitag
Vendredi
Viernes

II

Saturday

Samstag
Samedi
Sábado

I2

Sunday

Sonntag
Dimanche
Domingo

January

13

Monday

Montag
Lundi
Lunes

14

Tuesday

Dienstag
Mardi
Martes

15

Wednesday

Mittwoch
Mercredi
Miércoles

○

16

Thursday

Donnerstag
Jeudi
Jueves

17

Friday

Freitag
Vendredi
Viernes

18

Saturday

Samstag
Samedi
Sábado

19

Sunday

Sonntag
Dimanche
Domingo

January

Week 4 *Januar Janvier Enero*

20
Monday
Montag
Lundi
Lunes

USA *Martin Luther King Day*

21
Tuesday
Dienstag
Mardi
Martes

22
Wednesday
Mittwoch
Mercredi
Miércoles

23
Thursday
Donnerstag
Jeudi
Jueves

24
Friday
Freitag
Vendredi
Viernes

25
Saturday
Samstag
Samedi
Sábado

26
Sunday
Sonntag
Dimanche
Domingo

January / February

Januar Janvier Enero / Februar Février Febrero   **Week 5**

27

Monday

Montag
Lundi
Lunes

28

Tuesday

Dienstag
Mardi
Martes

29

Wednesday

Mittwoch
Mercredi
Miércoles

• **30**

Thursday

Donnerstag
Jeudi
Jueves

Chinese New Year

31

Friday

Freitag
Vendredi
Viernes

I

Saturday

Samstag
Samedi
Sábado

2

Sunday

Sonntag
Dimanche
Domingo

February

3 **Monday**
Montag
Lundi
Lunes

4 **Tuesday**
Dienstag
Mardi
Martes

5 **Wednesday**
Mittwoch
Mercredi
Miércoles

6 **Thursday**
Donnerstag
Jeudi
Jueves

7 **Friday**
Freitag
Vendredi
Viernes

8 **Saturday**
Samstag
Samedi
Sábado

9 **Sunday**
Sonntag
Dimanche
Domingo

February

IO
Monday

Montag
Lundi
Lunes

II
Tuesday

Dienstag
Mardi
Martes

I2
Wednesday

Mittwoch
Mercredi
Miércoles

I3
Thursday

Donnerstag
Jeudi
Jueves

St. Valentine's Day

○
I4
Friday

Freitag
Vendredi
Viernes

I5
Saturday

Samstag
Samedi
Sábado

I6
Sunday

Sonntag
Dimanche
Domingo

February

17 **Monday**   (USA) *President's Day*
Montag
Lundi
Lunes

18 **Tuesday**
Dienstag
Mardi
Martes

19 **Wednesday**
Mittwoch
Mercredi
Miércoles

20 **Thursday**
Donnerstag
Jeudi
Jueves

21 **Friday**
Freitag
Vendredi
Viernes

22 **Saturday**
Samstag
Samedi
Sábado

23 **Sunday**
Sonntag
Dimanche
Domingo

February / March

Februar Février Febrero / März Mars Marzo   **Week 9**

Monday 24

Montag
Lundi
Lunes

Tuesday 25

Dienstag
Mardi
Martes

Wednesday 26

Mittwoch
Mercredi
Miércoles

Thursday 27

Donnerstag
Jeudi
Jueves

Friday 28

Freitag
Vendredi
Viernes

●

Saturday 1

Samstag
Samedi
Sábado

Sunday 2

Sonntag
Dimanche
Domingo

March

Week 10 *März Mars Marzo*

3
Monday
Montag
Lundi
Lunes

Rosenmontag

4
Tuesday
Dienstag
Mardi
Martes

5
Wednesday
Mittwoch
Mercredi
Miércoles

6
Thursday
Donnerstag
Jeudi
Jueves

7
Friday
Freitag
Vendredi
Viernes

8
Saturday
Samstag
Samedi
Sábado

9
Sunday
Sonntag
Dimanche
Domingo

March

Monday — **IO**

Montag
Lundi
Lunes

Tuesday — **II**

Dienstag
Mardi
Martes

Wednesday — **I2**

Mittwoch
Mercredi
Miércoles

Thursday — **I3**

Donnerstag
Jeudi
Jueves

Friday — **I4**

Freitag
Vendredi
Viernes

Saturday — **I5**

Samstag
Samedi
Sábado

○ **Sunday** — **I6**

Sonntag
Dimanche
Domingo

March

17 **Monday**
Montag
Lundi
Lunes

Saint Patrick's Day

18 **Tuesday**
Dienstag
Mardi
Martes

19 **Wednesday**
Mittwoch
Mercredi
Miércoles

20 **Thursday**
Donnerstag
Jeudi
Jueves

21 **Friday**
Freitag
Vendredi
Viernes

22 **Saturday**
Samstag
Samedi
Sábado

23 **Sunday**
Sonntag
Dimanche
Domingo

Monday 24
Montag
Lundi
Lunes

Tuesday 25
Dienstag
Mardi
Martes

Wednesday 26
Mittwoch
Mercredi
Miércoles

Thursday 27
Donnerstag
Jeudi
Jueves

Friday 28
Freitag
Vendredi
Viernes

Saturday 29
Samstag
Samedi
Sábado

Sunday 30
Sonntag
Dimanche
Domingo

March / April

3I
Monday

Montag
Lundi
Lunes

I
Tuesday

Dienstag
Mardi
Martes

2
Wednesday

Mittwoch
Mercredi
Miércoles

3
Thursday

Donnerstag
Jeudi
Jueves

4
Friday

Freitag
Vendredi
Viernes

5
Saturday

Samstag
Samedi
Sábado

6
Sunday

Sonntag
Dimanche
Domingo

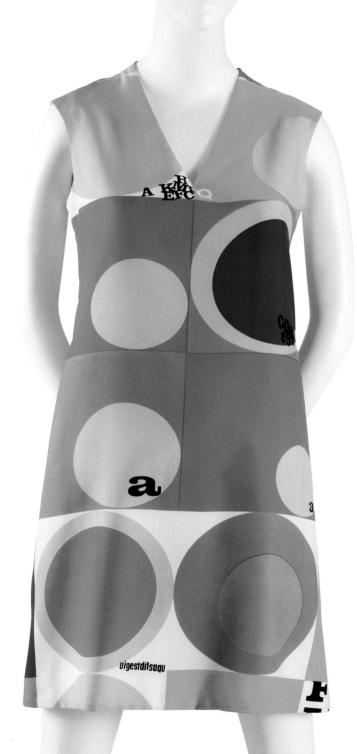

April

◖ **7**
Monday

Montag
Lundi
Lunes

8
Tuesday

Dienstag
Mardi
Martes

9
Wednesday

Mittwoch
Mercredi
Miércoles

10
Thursday

Donnerstag
Jeudi
Jueves

11
Friday

Freitag
Vendredi
Viernes

12
Saturday

Samstag
Samedi
Sábado

13
Sunday

Sonntag
Dimanche
Domingo

April

April Avril Abril

14
Monday
Montag
Lundi
Lunes

15
○   *First Day of Passover*
Tuesday
Dienstag
Mardi
Martes

16
Wednesday
Mittwoch
Mercredi
Miércoles

17
Thursday
Donnerstag
Jeudi
Jueves

18
                                                                (UK) (D) (E)
Friday   *Good Friday | Karfreitag |*
Freitag   *Viernes Santo*
Vendredi
Viernes

19
Saturday
Samstag
Samedi
Sábado

20
                                                                (UK) (D) (F) (E)
Sunday   *Easter Sunday | Ostersonntag |*
Sonntag   *Pâques | Pascua*
Dimanche
Domingo

April

UK D F

Easter Monday (except Scotland) |
Ostermontag | Lundi de Pâques

Monday **21**

Montag
Lundi
Lunes

◗ **Tuesday** **22**

Dienstag
Mardi
Martes

Wednesday **23**

Mittwoch
Mercredi
Miércoles

Thursday **24**

Donnerstag
Jeudi
Jueves

Friday **25**

Freitag
Vendredi
Viernes

Saturday **26**

Samstag
Samedi
Sábado

Sunday **27**

Sonntag
Dimanche
Domingo

April / May

Week 18

April Avril Abril / Mai Mai Mayo

28 Monday
Montag
Lundi
Lunes

29 Tuesday
●
Dienstag
Mardi
Martes

30 Wednesday
Mittwoch
Mercredi
Miércoles

1 Thursday
Donnerstag
Jeudi
Jueves

(D) (F) (E)
Tag der Arbeit | Fête du Travail |
Fiesta del Trabajo
May Day

2 Friday
Freitag
Vendredi
Viernes

3 Saturday
Samstag
Samedi
Sábado

4 Sunday
Sonntag
Dimanche
Domingo

May

(UK) *Early May Bank Holiday*

Monday   5

Montag
Lundi
Lunes

Tuesday   6

Dienstag
Mardi
Martes

☾

Wednesday   7

Mittwoch
Mercredi
Miércoles

(F) *Fête de la Libération*

Thursday   8

Donnerstag
Jeudi
Jueves

Friday   9

Freitag
Vendredi
Viernes

Saturday   10

Samstag
Samedi
Sábado

Mother's Day

Sunday   11

Sonntag
Dimanche
Domingo

May

Mai Mai Mayo

12
Monday

Montag
Lundi
Lunes

13
Tuesday

Dienstag
Mardi
Martes

14
○
Wednesday

Mittwoch
Mercredi
Miércoles

15
Thursday

Donnerstag
Jeudi
Jueves

16
Friday

Freitag
Vendredi
Viernes

17
Saturday

Samstag
Samedi
Sábado

18
Sunday

Sonntag
Dimanche
Domingo

May

Mai Mai Mayo   **Week 21**

19
Monday
Montag
Lundi
Lunes

20
Tuesday
Dienstag
Mardi
Martes

21
Wednesday
Mittwoch
Mercredi
Miércoles

22
Thursday
Donnerstag
Jeudi
Jueves

23
Friday
Freitag
Vendredi
Viernes

24
Saturday
Samstag
Samedi
Sábado

25
Sunday
Sonntag
Dimanche
Domingo

May / June

Week 22 *Mai Mai Mayo / Juni Juin Junio*

26
Monday

Montag
Lundi
Lunes

(USA) *Memorial Day*
(UK) *Spring Bank Holiday*

27
Tuesday

Dienstag
Mardi
Martes

---

28 •
Wednesday

Mittwoch
Mercredi
Miércoles

29
Thursday

Donnerstag
Jeudi
Jueves

(D) (F) *Christi Himmelfahrt | Ascension*

30
Friday

Freitag
Vendredi
Viernes

31
Saturday

Samstag
Samedi
Sábado

I
Sunday

Sonntag
Dimanche
Domingo

June

Juni Juin Junio   **Week 23**

Monday   **2**

Montag
Lundi
Lunes

Tuesday   **3**

Dienstag
Mardi
Martes

Wednesday   **4**

Mittwoch
Mercredi
Miércoles

☾
Thursday   **5**

Donnerstag
Jeudi
Jueves

Friday   **6**

Freitag
Vendredi
Viernes

Saturday   **7**

Samstag
Samedi
Sábado

Ⓓ Ⓕ *Pfingstsonntag | Pentecôte*

Sunday   **8**

Sonntag
Dimanche
Domingo

June

9

Monday

Montag
Lundi
Lunes

ⒹⒻ *Pfingstmontag | Lundi de Pentecôte*

10

Tuesday

Dienstag
Mardi
Martes

11

Wednesday

Mittwoch
Mercredi
Miércoles

12

Thursday

Donnerstag
Jeudi
Jueves

13

○
Friday

Freitag
Vendredi
Viernes

14

Saturday

Samstag
Samedi
Sábado

15

Sunday

Sonntag
Dimanche
Domingo

June

16

Monday

Montag
Lundi
Lunes

17

Tuesday

Dienstag
Mardi
Martes

18

Wednesday

Mittwoch
Mercredi
Miércoles

Ⓓ *Fronleichnam (teilw.)*

◗ **19**

Thursday

Donnerstag
Jeudi
Jueves

20

Friday

Freitag
Vendredi
Viernes

21

Saturday

Samstag
Samedi
Sábado

22

Sunday

Sonntag
Dimanche
Domingo

June

23   **Monday**
Montag
Lundi
Lunes

24   **Tuesday**
Dienstag
Mardi
Martes

25   **Wednesday**
Mittwoch
Mercredi
Miércoles

26   **Thursday**
Donnerstag
Jeudi
Jueves

27   ●
Friday
Freitag
Vendredi
Viernes

First Day of Ramadan

28   **Saturday**
Samstag
Samedi
Sábado

29   **Sunday**
Sonntag
Dimanche
Domingo

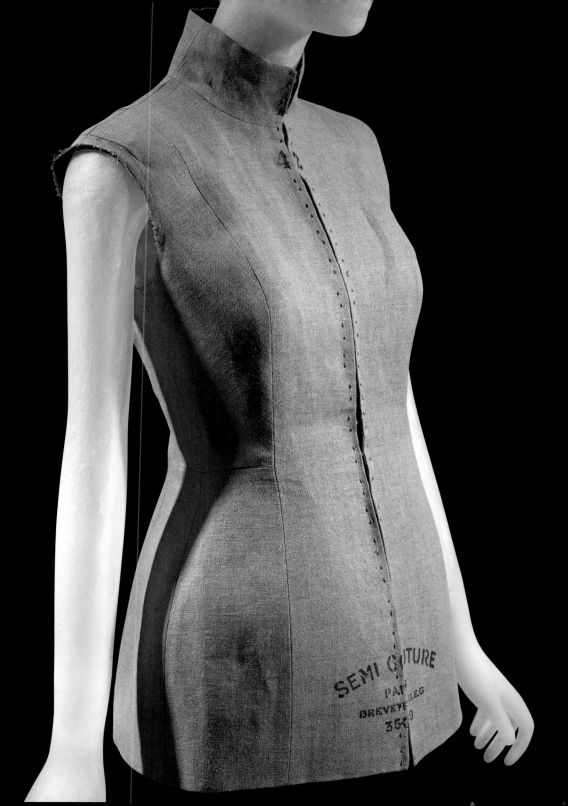

Monday   3O

Montag
Lundi
Lunes

Tuesday   I

Dienstag
Mardi
Martes

Wednesday   2

Mittwoch
Mercredi
Miércoles

Thursday   3

Donnerstag
Jeudi
Jueves

(USA) *Independence Day*

Friday   4

Freitag
Vendredi
Viernes

◐

Saturday   5

Samstag
Samedi
Sábado

Sunday   6

Sonntag
Dimanche
Domingo

July

Juli Juillet Julio

7
Monday

Montag
Lundi
Lunes

8
Tuesday

Dienstag
Mardi
Martes

9
Wednesday

Mittwoch
Mercredi
Miércoles

10
Thursday

Donnerstag
Jeudi
Jueves

11
Friday

Freitag
Vendredi
Viernes

12
○

Saturday

Samstag
Samedi
Sábado

(UK) *Battle of the Boyne Day (Northern Ireland only)*

13
Sunday

Sonntag
Dimanche
Domingo

July

Juli Juillet Julio   **Week 29**

(UK) *Public Holiday (Northern Ireland only)*
(F) *Fête Nationale*

Monday   **14**

Montag
Lundi
Lunes

Tuesday   **15**

Dienstag
Mardi
Martes

Wednesday   **16**

Mittwoch
Mercredi
Miércoles

Thursday   **17**

Donnerstag
Jeudi
Jueves

Friday   **18**

Freitag
Vendredi
Viernes

Saturday   **19**

Samstag
Samedi
Sábado

Sunday   **20**

Sonntag
Dimanche
Domingo

July

21
Monday

Montag
Lundi
Lunes

22
Tuesday

Dienstag
Mardi
Martes

23
Wednesday

Mittwoch
Mercredi
Miércoles

24
Thursday

Donnerstag
Jeudi
Jueves

25
Friday

Freitag
Vendredi
Viernes

26
●
Saturday

Samstag
Samedi
Sábado

27
Sunday

Sonntag
Dimanche
Domingo

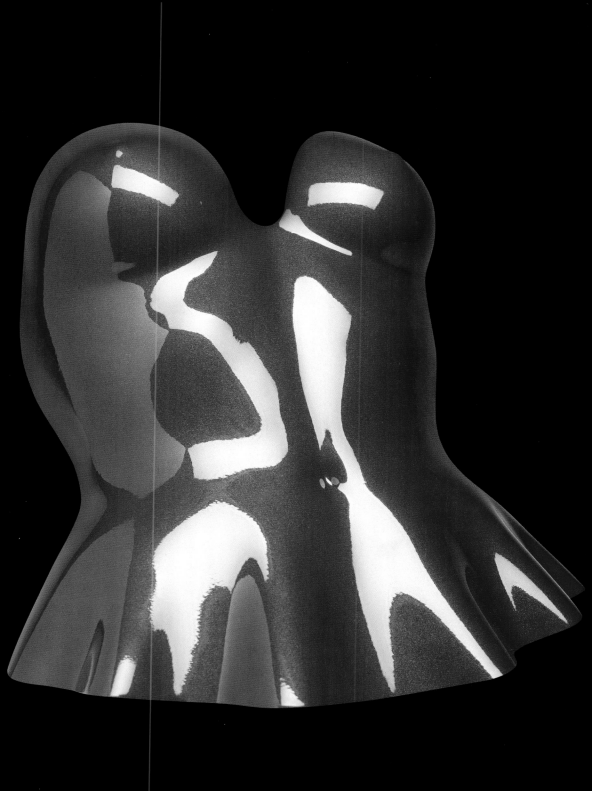

Last Day of Ramadan

Monday 28
Montag
Lundi
Lunes

Tuesday 29
Dienstag
Mardi
Martes

Wednesday 30
Mittwoch
Mercredi
Miércoles

Thursday 31
Donnerstag
Jeudi
Jueves

Friday 1
Freitag
Vendredi
Viernes

Saturday 2
Samstag
Samedi
Sábado

Sunday 3
Sonntag
Dimanche
Domingo

August

4 ◗	**Monday** *Montag* *Lundi* *Lunes*	UK *Summer Bank Holiday (Scotland only)*
5	**Tuesday** *Dienstag* *Mardi* *Martes*	
6	**Wednesday** *Mittwoch* *Mercredi* *Miércoles*	
7	**Thursday** *Donnerstag* *Jeudi* *Jueves*	
8	**Friday** *Freitag* *Vendredi* *Viernes*	
9	**Saturday** *Samstag* *Samedi* *Sábado*	
10 ○	**Sunday** *Sonntag* *Dimanche* *Domingo*	

August

Monday **II**
Montag
Lundi
Lunes

Tuesday **I2**
Dienstag
Mardi
Martes

Wednesday **I3**
Mittwoch
Mercredi
Miércoles

Thursday **I4**
Donnerstag
Jeudi
Jueves

Ⓓ Ⓕ Ⓔ
Mariä Himmelfahrt (teilw.) | Assomption |
Asunción de la Virgen

Friday **I5**
Freitag
Vendredi
Viernes

Saturday **I6**
Samstag
Samedi
Sábado

◗
Sunday **I7**
Sonntag
Dimanche
Domingo

August

18
Monday

Montag
Lundi
Lunes

19
Tuesday

Dienstag
Mardi
Martes

20
Wednesday

Mittwoch
Mercredi
Miércoles

21
Thursday

Donnerstag
Jeudi
Jueves

22
Friday

Freitag
Vendredi
Viernes

23
Saturday

Samstag
Samedi
Sábado

24
Sunday

Sonntag
Dimanche
Domingo

August

UK *Summer Bank Holiday (except Scotland)*

● **Monday** 25

Montag
Lundi
Lunes

Tuesday 26

Dienstag
Mardi
Martes

Wednesday 27

Mittwoch
Mercredi
Miércoles

Thursday 28

Donnerstag
Jeudi
Jueves

Friday 29

Freitag
Vendredi
Viernes

Saturday 30

Samstag
Samedi
Sábado

Sunday 31

Sonntag
Dimanche
Domingo

September

September Septembre Septiembre

1 **Monday**

Montag
Lundi
Lunes

(USA) *Labor Day*

2 **Tuesday**

Dienstag
Mardi
Martes

3 **Wednesday**

Mittwoch
Mercredi
Miércoles

4 **Thursday**

Donnerstag
Jeudi
Jueves

5 **Friday**

Freitag
Vendredi
Viernes

6 **Saturday**

Samstag
Samedi
Sábado

7 **Sunday**

Sonntag
Dimanche
Domingo

September

8

Monday

Montag
Lundi
Lunes

○

9

Tuesday

Dienstag
Mardi
Martes

10

Wednesday

Mittwoch
Mercredi
Miércoles

11

Thursday

Donnerstag
Jeudi
Jueves

12

Friday

Freitag
Vendredi
Viernes

13

Saturday

Samstag
Samedi
Sábado

14

Sunday

Sonntag
Dimanche
Domingo

15
Monday

Montag
Lundi
Lunes

16
Tuesday

Dienstag
Mardi
Martes

17
Wednesday

Mittwoch
Mercredi
Miércoles

18
Thursday

Donnerstag
Jeudi
Jueves

19
Friday

Freitag
Vendredi
Viernes

20
Saturday

Samstag
Samedi
Sábado

21
Sunday

Sonntag
Dimanche
Domingo

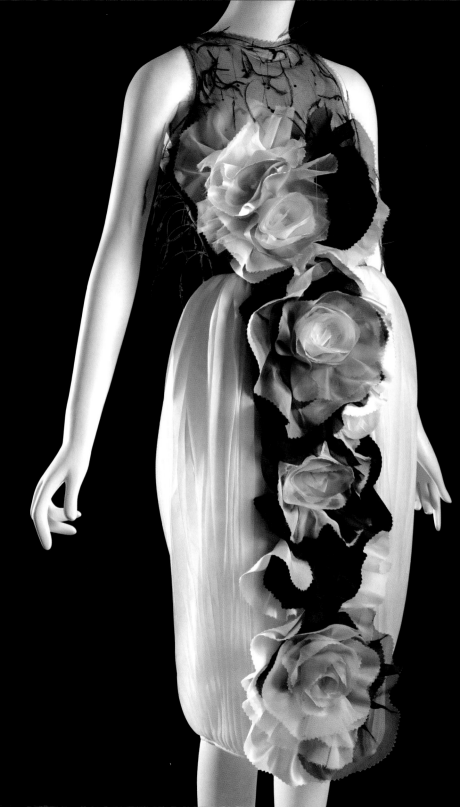

Monday 22
Montag
Lundi
Lunes

Tuesday 23
Dienstag
Mardi
Martes

●
Wednesday 24
Mittwoch
Mercredi
Miércoles

Jewish New Year

Thursday 25
Donnerstag
Jeudi
Jueves

Friday 26
Freitag
Vendredi
Viernes

Saturday 27
Samstag
Samedi
Sábado

Sunday 28
Sonntag
Dimanche
Domingo

September / October

September Septembre Septiembre / Oktober Octobre Octubre

29 Monday
Montag
Lundi
Lunes

30 Tuesday
Dienstag
Mardi
Martes

1 Wednesday
Mittwoch
Mercredi
Miércoles

2 Thursday
Donnerstag
Jeudi
Jueves

Tag der Deutschen Einheit

3 Friday
Freitag
Vendredi
Viernes

Yom Kippur

4 Saturday
Samstag
Samedi
Sábado

5 Sunday
Sonntag
Dimanche
Domingo

October

6

Monday

Montag
Lundi
Lunes

7

Tuesday

Dienstag
Mardi
Martes

○

8

Wednesday

Mittwoch
Mercredi
Miércoles

9

Thursday

Donnerstag
Jeudi
Jueves

10

Friday

Freitag
Vendredi
Viernes

11

Saturday

Samstag
Samedi
Sábado

Ⓔ *Fiesta Nacional*

12

Sunday

Sonntag
Dimanche
Domingo

October

Oktober Octobre Octubre

13
Monday

Montag
Lundi
Lunes

(USA) *Columbus Day*

14
Tuesday

Dienstag
Mardi
Martes

15
Wednesday

Mittwoch
Mercredi
Miércoles

16
Thursday

Donnerstag
Jeudi
Jueves

17
Friday

Freitag
Vendredi
Viernes

18
Saturday

Samstag
Samedi
Sábado

19
Sunday

Sonntag
Dimanche
Domingo

October

Oktober Octobre Octubre   **Week 43**

20 **Monday**
Montag
Lundi
Lunes

21 **Tuesday**
Dienstag
Mardi
Martes

22 **Wednesday**
Mittwoch
Mercredi
Miércoles

• **23** **Thursday**
Donnerstag
Jeudi
Jueves

24 **Friday**
Freitag
Vendredi
Viernes

Islamic New Year

25 **Saturday**
Samstag
Samedi
Sábado

26 **Sunday**
Sonntag
Dimanche
Domingo

27 **Monday**
Montag
Lundi
Lunes

28 **Tuesday**
Dienstag
Mardi
Martes

29 **Wednesday**
Mittwoch
Mercredi
Miércoles

30 **Thursday**
Donnerstag
Jeudi
Jueves

31 ◗ **Friday**
Freitag
Vendredi
Viernes

ⓓ *Reformationstag (teilw.)*
Halloween

1 **Saturday**
Samstag
Samedi
Sábado

ⓓ ⓕ ⓔ
Allerheiligen (teilw.) | Toussaint |
Todos los Santos

2 **Sunday**
Sonntag
Dimanche
Domingo

November

November Novembre Noviembre **Week 45**

Monday   3

Montag
Lundi
Lunes

Tuesday   4

Dienstag
Mardi
Martes

Wednesday   5

Mittwoch
Mercredi
Miércoles

○

Thursday   6

Donnerstag
Jeudi
Jueves

Friday   7

Freitag
Vendredi
Viernes

Saturday   8

Samstag
Samedi
Sábado

Sunday   9

Sonntag
Dimanche
Domingo

November

Week 46 *November Novembre Noviembre*

IO
Monday
Montag
Lundi
Lunes

II
Tuesday
Dienstag
Mardi
Martes

(USA) *Veterans' Day*
(F) *Armistice 1918*

I2
Wednesday
Mittwoch
Mercredi
Miércoles

I3
Thursday
Donnerstag
Jeudi
Jueves

I4
◗
Friday
Freitag
Vendredi
Viernes

I5
Saturday
Samstag
Samedi
Sábado

I6
Sunday
Sonntag
Dimanche
Domingo

November

Monday   **17**
Montag
Lundi
Lunes

Tuesday   **18**
Dienstag
Mardi
Martes

Ⓓ *Buß- und Bettag (teilw.)*

Wednesday   **19**
Mittwoch
Mercredi
Miércoles

Thursday   **20**
Donnerstag
Jeudi
Jueves

Friday   **21**
Freitag
Vendredi
Viernes

● **Saturday**   **22**
Samstag
Samedi
Sábado

Sunday   **23**
Sonntag
Dimanche
Domingo

November

Week 48 *November Novembre Noviembre*

24
Monday

Montag
Lundi
Lunes

25
Tuesday

Dienstag
Mardi
Martes

26
Wednesday

Mittwoch
Mercredi
Miércoles

27
(USA) Thanksgiving Day

Thursday

Donnerstag
Jeudi
Jueves

28
Friday

Freitag
Vendredi
Viernes

29
Saturday

Samstag
Samedi
Sábado

30
(UK) Saint Andrew's Day (Scotland only)

Sunday

Sonntag
Dimanche
Domingo

December

Dezember Décembre Diciembre   **Week 49**

(UK) *Public Holiday (Scotland only)*

Monday 1

Montag
Lundi
Lunes

Tuesday 2

Dienstag
Mardi
Martes

Wednesday 3

Mittwoch
Mercredi
Miércoles

Thursday 4

Donnerstag
Jeudi
Jueves

Friday 5

Freitag
Vendredi
Viernes

(E) *Día de la Constitución*

○
Saturday 6

Samstag
Samedi
Sábado

Sunday 7

Sonntag
Dimanche
Domingo

December

Week 50 *Dezember Décembre Diciembre*

8
Monday

Montag
Lundi
Lunes

Ⓔ *Inmaculada Concepción*

9
Tuesday

Dienstag
Mardi
Martes

10
Wednesday

Mittwoch
Mercredi
Miércoles

11
Thursday

Donnerstag
Jeudi
Jueves

12
Friday

Freitag
Vendredi
Viernes

13
Saturday

Samstag
Samedi
Sábado

14
Sunday

Sonntag
Dinanche
Domingo

Monday — *Montag / Lundi / Lunes*   **15**

Tuesday — *Dienstag / Mardi / Martes*   **16**

First Day of Hanukkah

Wednesday — *Mittwoch / Mercredi / Miércoles*   **17**

Thursday — *Donnerstag / Jeudi / Jueves*   **18**

Friday — *Freitag / Vendredi / Viernes*   **19**

Saturday — *Samstag / Samedi / Sábado*   **20**

Sunday — *Sonntag / Dimanche / Domingo*   **21**

December

Dezember Décembre Diciembre

22
Monday

Montag
Lundi
Lunes

23
Tuesday

Dienstag
Mardi
Martes

24
Wednesday

Mittwoch
Mercredi
Miércoles

25
Thursday

Donnerstag
Jeudi
Jueves

(USA) (UK) (D) (F) (E)

Christmas Day | 1. Weihnachtstag |
Noël | Natividad del Señor

26
Friday

Freitag
Vendredi
Viernes

(UK) (D) *Boxing Day | 2. Weihnachtstag*

27
Saturday

Samstag
Samedi
Sábado

28
Sunday

Sonntag
Dimanche
Domingo

December / January

Monday 29
Montag
Lundi
Lunes

Tuesday 30
Dienstag
Mardi
Martes

Wednesday 31
Mittwoch
Mercredi
Miércoles

(USA) (UK) (D) (F) (E)
New Year's Day | Neujahr |
Jour de l'An | Año Nuevo

Thursday 1
Donnerstag
Jeudi
Jueves

(UK) *Public Holiday (Scotland only)*

Friday 2
Freitag
Vendredi
Viernes

Saturday 3
Samstag
Samedi
Sábado

Sunday 4
Sonntag
Dimanche
Domingo

Public Holidays 2014

Ⓐ Österreich
1.1 Neujahr
6.1 Heilige Drei Könige
20.4 Ostersonntag
21.4 Ostermontag
1.5 Staatsfeiertag
29.5 Christi Himmelfahrt
8.6 Pfingstsonntag
9.6 Pfingstmontag
19.6 Fronleichnam
15.8 Mariä Himmelfahrt
26.10 Nationalfeiertag
1.11 Allerheiligen
8.12 Mariä Empfängnis
25.12 Weihnachten
26.12 Stephanstag

Ⓑ Belgique / België
1.1 Jour de l'An / Nieuwjaar
20.4 Pâques / Pasen
21.4 Lundi de Pâques / Paasmaandag
1.5 Fête du Travail / Feest van de Arbeid
29.5 Ascension / Onze-Lieve-Heer-Hemelvaart
8.6 Pentecôte / Pinksteren
9.6 Lundi de Pentecôte / Pinkstermaandag
21.7 Fête Nationale / Nationale Feestdag
15.8 Assomption / Onze-Lieve-Vrouw-Hemelvaart
1.11 Toussaint / Allerheiligen
11.11 Armistice / Wapenstilstand
25.12 Noël / Kerstmis

ⒸⒹⓃ Canada
1.1 New Year's Day / Jour de l'An
18.4 Good Friday / Vendredi Saint
20.4 Easter Sunday / Pâques
21.4 Easter Monday / Lundi de Pâques
19.5 Victoria Day / Fête de la Reine
1.7 Canada Day / Fête du Canada
1.9 Labour Day / Fête du Travail
13.10 Thanksgiving Day / Action de Grâces
11.11 Remembrance Day / Jour du Souvenir
25.12 Christmas Day / Noël
26.12 Boxing Day / Lendemain de Noël

Ⓒⓗ Schweiz / Suisse / Svizzera
1.1 Neujahr / Nouvel An / Capodanno
18.4 Karfreitag / Vendredi Saint / Venerdì Santo
20.4 Ostern / Pâques / Pasqua
21.4 Ostermontag / Lundi de Pâques / Lunedì di Pasqua

29.5 Auffahrt / Ascension / Ascensione
8.6 Pfingstsonntag / Pentecôte / Pentecoste
9.6 Pfingstmontag / Lundi de Pentecôte / Lunedì di Pentecoste
1.8 Bundesfeiertag / Fête Nationale / Festa Nazionale
25.12 Weihnachten / Noël / Natale
26.12 Stefanstag / S. Etienne / S. Stefano

Ⓓ Bundesrepublik Deutschland
1.1 Neujahr
6.1 Heilige Drei Könige (teilw.)
18.4 Karfreitag
20.4 Ostersonntag
21.4 Ostermontag
1.5 Tag der Arbeit
29.5 Christi Himmelfahrt
8.6 Pfingstsonntag
9.6 Pfingstmontag
19.6 Fronleichnam (teilw.)
15.8 Mariä Himmelfahrt (teilw.)
3.10 Tag der Deutschen Einheit
31.10 Reformationstag (teilw.)
1.11 Allerheiligen (teilw.)
19.11 Buß- und Bettag (teilw.)
25.12 1. Weihnachtstag
26.12 2. Weihnachtstag

Ⓔ España
1.1 Año Nuevo
6.1 Reyes
18.4 Viernes Santo
20.4 Pascua
1.5 Fiesta del Trabajo
15.8 Asunción de la Virgen
12.10 Fiesta Nacional
1.11 Todos los Santos
6.12 Día de la Constitución
8.12 Inmaculada Concepción
25.12 Natividad del Señor

Ⓕ France
1.1 Jour de l'An
20.4 Pâques
21.4 Lundi de Pâques
1.5 Fête du Travail
8.5 Fête de la Libération
29.5 Ascension
8.6 Pentecôte
9.6 Lundi de Pentecôte
14.7 Fête Nationale
15.8 Assomption
1.11 Toussaint
11.11 Armistice 1918
25.12 Noël

Ⓘ Italia
1.1 Capodanno
6.1 Epifania
20.4 Pasqua
21.4 Lunedì dell'Angelo
25.4 Liberazione
1.5 Festa del Lavoro
2.6 Festa della Repubblica
15.8 Assunzione
1.11 Ognissanti
8.12 Immacolata Concezione
25.12 Natale
26.12 S. Stefano

ⒾⓇⓁ Ireland
1.1 New Year's Day
17.3 Saint Patrick's Day
20.4 Easter Sunday
21.4 Easter Monday
5.5 First Monday in May
2.6 First Monday in June
4.8 First Monday in August
27.10 Last Monday in October
25.12 Christmas Day
26.12 Saint Stephen's Day

Ⓙ Japan
1.1 New Year's Day
13.1 Coming-of-Age Day
11.2 Commemoration of the Founding of the Nation
21.3 Vernal Equinox Day
29.4 Showa's Day
3.5 Constitution Day
4.5 Greenery Day
5.5 Children's Day
6.5 Public Holiday
21.7 Marine Day
15.9 Respect-for-the-Aged Day
23.9 Autumn Equinox Day
13.10 Health-Sports Day
3.11 Culture Day
23.11 Labor-Thanksgiving Day
24.11 Public Holiday
23.12 Emperor's Birthday

ⓃⓁ Nederland
1.1 Nieuwjaarsdag
20.4 1e Paasdag
21.4 2e Paasdag
30.4 Koninginnedag
29.5 Hemelvaartsdag
8.6 1e Pinksterdag
9.6 2e Pinksterdag
25.12 1e Kerstdag
26.12 2e Kerstdag

Ⓟ Portugal
1.1 Ano Novo
18.4 Sexta-feira Santa
20.4 Domingo de Páscoa
25.4 Dia da Liberdade
1.5 Dia do Trabalho
10.6 Dia Nacional
19.6 Corpo de Deus
15.8 Assunção de Nossa Senhora
5.10 Implantação da República
1.11 Todos os Santos
1.12 Dia da Restauração
8.12 Imaculada Conceição
25.12 Dia de Natal

ⓊⓀ United Kingdom
1.1 New Year's Day
2.1 Public Holiday (Scotland only)
17.3 Saint Patrick's Day (Northern Ireland only)
18.4 Good Friday
20.4 Easter Sunday
21.4 Easter Monday (except Scotland)
5.5 Early May Bank Holiday
26.5 Spring Bank Holiday
12.7 Battle of the Boyne Day (Northern Ireland only)
14.7 Public Holiday (Northern Ireland only)
4.8 Summer Bank Holiday (Scotland only)
25.8 Summer Bank Holiday (except Scotland)
30.11 Saint Andrew's Day (Scotland only)
1.12 Public Holiday (Scotland only)
25.12 Christmas Day
26.12 Boxing Day

ⓊⓈⒶ United States
1.1 New Year's Day
20.1 Martin Luther King Day
17.2 President's Day
26.5 Memorial Day
4.7 Independence Day
1.9 Labor Day
13.10 Columbus Day
11.11 Veterans' Day
27.11 Thanksgiving Day
25.12 Christmas Day

Some international holidays may be subject to change.

Credits

Year Planner

September	October	November	December
1 Su	1 Tu	1 Fr	1 Su
Week 36	2 We	2 Sa	*Week 49*
2 Mo	3 Th	3 Su ●	2 Mo
3 Tu	4 Fr	*Week 45*	3 Tu ●
4 We	5 Sa ●	4 Mo	4 We
5 Th ●	6 Su	5 Tu	5 Th
6 Fr	*Week 41*	6 We	6 Fr
7 Sa	7 Mo	7 Th	7 Sa
8 Su	8 Tu	8 Fr	8 Su
Week 37	9 We	9 Sa	*Week 50*
9 Mo	10 Th	10 Su ◑	9 Mo ◑
10 Tu	11 Fr ◑	*Week 46*	10 Tu
11 We	12 Sa	11 Mo	11 We
12 Th ◑	13 Su	12 Tu	12 Th
13 Fr	*Week 42*	13 We	13 Fr
14 Sa	14 Mo	14 Th	14 Sa
15 Su	15 Tu	15 Fr	15 Su
Week 38	16 We	16 Sa	*Week 51*
16 Mo	17 Th	17 Su ○	16 Mo
17 Tu	18 Fr ○	*Week 47*	17 Tu ○
18 We	19 Sa	18 Mo	18 We
19 Th ○	20 Su	19 Tu	19 Th
20 Fr	*Week 43*	20 We	20 Fr
21 Sa	21 Mo	21 Th	21 Sa
22 Su	22 Tu	22 Fr	22 Su
Week 39	23 We	23 Sa	*Week 52*
23 Mo	24 Th	24 Su	23 Mo
24 Tu	25 Fr	*Week 48*	24 Tu
25 We	26 Sa ◐	25 Mo ◐	25 We ◐
26 Th	27 Su	26 Tu	26 Th
27 Fr ◐	*Week 44*	27 We	27 Fr
28 Sa	28 Mo	28 Th	28 Sa
29 Su	29 Tu	29 Fr	29 Su
Week 40	30 We	30 Sa	*Week 1*
30 Mo	31 Th		30 Mo
			31 Tu

Year Planner

January	February	March	April
1 We ●	1 Sa	1 Sa ●	1 Tu
2 Th	2 Su	2 Su	2 We
3 Fr	*Week 6*	*Week 10*	3 Th
4 Sa	3 Mo	3 Mo	4 Fr
5 Su	4 Tu	4 Tu	5 Sa
Week 2	5 We	5 We	6 Su
6 Mo	6 Th ◑	6 Th	*Week 15*
7 Tu	7 Fr	7 Fr	7 Mo ◑
8 We ◑	8 Sa	8 Sa ◑	8 Tu
9 Th	9 Su	9 Su	9 We
10 Fr	*Week 7*	*Week 11*	10 Th
11 Sa	10 Mo	10 Mo	11 Fr
12 Su	11 Tu	11 Tu	12 Sa
Week 3	12 We	12 We	13 Su
13 Mo	13 Th	13 Th	*Week 16*
14 Tu	14 Fr ○	14 Fr	14 Mo
15 We	15 Sa	15 Sa	15 Tu ○
16 Th ○	16 Su	16 Su ○	16 We
17 Fr	*Week 8*	*Week 12*	17 Th
18 Sa	17 Mo	17 Mo	18 Fr
19 Su	18 Tu	18 Tu	19 Sa
Week 4	19 We	19 We	20 Su
20 Mo	20 Th	20 Th	*Week 17*
21 Tu	21 Fr	21 Fr	21 Mo
22 We	22 Sa ◐	22 Sa	22 Tu ◐
23 Th	23 Su	23 Su	23 We
24 Fr ◐	*Week 9*	*Week 13*	24 Th
25 Sa	24 Mo	24 Mo ◐	25 Fr
26 Su	25 Tu	25 Tu	26 Sa
Week 5	26 We	26 We	27 Su
27 Mo	27 Th	27 Th	*Week 18*
28 Tu	28 Fr	28 Fr	28 Mo
29 We		29 Sa	29 Tu ●
30 Th ●		30 Su ●	30 We
31 Fr		*Week 14*	
		31 Mo	

May	June	July	August
1 Th	1 Su	1 Tu	1 Fr
2 Fr	**Week 23**	2 We	2 Sa
3 Sa	2 Mo	3 Th	3 Su
4 Su	3 Tu	4 Fr	**Week 32**
Week 19	4 We	5 Sa ◐	4 Mo ◐
5 Mo	5 Th ◐	6 Su	5 Tu
6 Tu	6 Fr	**Week 28**	6 We
7 We ◑	7 Sa	7 Mo	7 Th
8 Th	8 Su	8 Tu	8 Fr
9 Fr	**Week 24**	9 We	9 Sa
10 Sa	9 Mo	10 Th	10 Su ○
11 Su	10 Tu	11 Fr	**Week 33**
Week 20	11 We	12 Sa ○	11 Mo
12 Mo	12 Th	13 Su	12 Tu
13 Tu	13 Fr ○	**Week 29**	13 We
14 We ○	14 Sa	14 Mo	14 Th
15 Th	15 Su	15 Tu	15 Fr
16 Fr	**Week 25**	16 We	16 Sa
17 Sa	16 Mo	17 Th	17 Su ◑
18 Su	17 Tu	18 Fr	**Week 34**
Week 21	18 We	19 Sa ◑	18 Mo
19 Mo	19 Th ◑	20 Su	19 Tu
20 Tu	20 Fr	**Week 30**	20 We
21 We ◑	21 Sa	21 Mo	21 Th
22 Th	22 Su	22 Tu	22 Fr
23 Fr	**Week 26**	23 We	23 Sa
24 Sa	23 Mo	24 Th	24 Su
25 Su	24 Tu	25 Fr	**Week 35**
Week 22	25 We	26 Sa ●	25 Mo ●
26 Mo	26 Th	27 Su	26 Tu
27 Tu	27 Fr ●	**Week 31**	27 We
28 We ●	28 Sa	28 Mo	28 Th
29 Th	29 Su	29 Tu	29 Fr
30 Fr	**Week 27**	30 We	30 Sa
31 Sa	30 Mo	31 Th	31 Su

Year Planner

September

Week 36
1 Mo
2 Tu ◑
3 We
4 Th
5 Fr
6 Sa
7 Su

Week 37
8 Mo
9 Tu ○
10 We
11 Th
12 Fr
13 Sa
14 Su

Week 38
15 Mo
16 Tu ◐
17 We
18 Th
19 Fr
20 Sa
21 Su

Week 39
22 Mo
23 Tu
24 We ●
25 Th
26 Fr
27 Sa
28 Su

Week 40
29 Mo
30 Tu

October

1 We ◑
2 Th
3 Fr
4 Sa
5 Su

Week 41
6 Mo
7 Tu
8 We ○
9 Th
10 Fr
11 Sa
12 Su

Week 42
13 Mo
14 Tu
15 We ◐
16 Th
17 Fr
18 Sa
19 Su

Week 43
20 Mo
21 Tu
22 We
23 Th ●
24 Fr
25 Sa
26 Su

Week 44
27 Mo
28 Tu
29 We
30 Th
31 Fr ◑

November

1 Sa
2 Su

Week 45
3 Mo
4 Tu
5 We
6 Th ○
7 Fr
8 Sa
9 Su

Week 46
10 Mo
11 Tu
12 We
13 Th
14 Fr ◐
15 Sa
16 Su

Week 47
17 Mo
18 Tu
19 We
20 Th
21 Fr
22 Sa ●
23 Su

Week 48
24 Mo
25 Tu
26 We
27 Th
28 Fr
29 Sa ◑
30 Su

December

Week 49
1 Mo
2 Tu
3 We
4 Th
5 Fr
6 Sa ○
7 Su

Week 50
8 Mo
9 Tu
10 We
11 Th
12 Fr
13 Sa
14 Su ◐

Week 51
15 Mo
16 Tu
17 We
18 Th
19 Fr
20 Sa
21 Su

Week 52
22 Mo ●
23 Tu
24 We
25 Th
26 Fr
27 Sa
28 Su ◑

Week 1
29 Mo
30 Tu
31 We

January

1	Th
2	Fr
3	Sa
4	Su
Week 2	
5	Mo ○
6	Tu
7	We
8	Th
9	Fr
10	Sa
11	Su
Week 3	
12	Mo
13	Tu ◑
14	We
15	Th
16	Fr
17	Sa
18	Su
Week 4	
19	Mo
20	Tu ●
21	We
22	Th
23	Fr
24	Sa
25	Su
Week 5	
26	Mo
27	Tu ◐
28	We
29	Th
30	Fr
31	Sa

February

1	Su
Week 6	
2	Mo
3	Tu ○
4	We
5	Th
6	Fr
7	Sa
8	Su
Week 7	
9	Mo
10	Tu
11	We
12	Th ◑
13	Fr
14	Sa
15	Su
Week 8	
16	Mo
17	Tu
18	We ●
19	Th
20	Fr
21	Sa
22	Su
Week 9	
23	Mo
24	Tu
25	We ◐
26	Th
27	Fr
28	Sa

March

1	Su
Week 10	
2	Mo
3	Tu
4	We
5	Th ○
6	Fr
7	Sa
8	Su
Week 11	
9	Mo
10	Tu
11	We
12	Th
13	Fr ◑
14	Sa
15	Su
Week 12	
16	Mo
17	Tu
18	We
19	Th
20	Fr ●
21	Sa
22	Su
Week 13	
23	Mo
24	Tu
25	We
26	Th
27	Fr ◐
28	Sa
29	Su
Week 14	
30	Mo
31	Tu

April

1	We
2	Th
3	Fr
4	Sa ○
5	Su
Week 15	
6	Mo
7	Tu
8	We
9	Th
10	Fr
11	Sa
12	Su ◑
Week 16	
13	Mo
14	Tu
15	We
16	Th
17	Fr
18	Sa ●
19	Su
Week 17	
20	Mo
21	Tu
22	We
23	Th
24	Fr
25	Sa ◐
26	Su
Week 18	
27	Mo
28	Tu
29	We
30	Th

Year Planner

May	June	July	August
1 Fr	*Week 23*	1 We	1 Sa
2 Sa	1 Mo	2 Th ○	2 Su
3 Su	2 Tu ○	3 Fr	*Week 32*
Week 19	3 We	4 Sa	3 Mo
4 Mo ○	4 Th	5 Su	4 Tu
5 Tu	5 Fr	*Week 28*	5 We
6 We	6 Sa	6 Mo	6 Th
7 Th	7 Su	7 Tu	7 Fr ◑
8 Fr	*Week 24*	8 We ◑	8 Sa
9 Sa	8 Mo	9 Th	9 Su
10 Su	9 Tu ◑	10 Fr	*Week 33*
Week 20	10 We	11 Sa	10 Mo
11 Mo ◑	11 Th	12 Su	11 Tu
12 Tu	12 Fr	*Week 29*	12 We
13 We	13 Sa	13 Mo	13 Th
14 Th	14 Su	14 Tu	14 Fr ●
15 Fr	*Week 25*	15 We	15 Sa
16 Sa	15 Mo	16 Th ●	16 Su
17 Su	16 Tu ●	17 Fr	*Week 34*
Week 21	17 We	18 Sa	17 Mo
18 Mo ●	18 Th	19 Su	18 Tu
19 Tu	19 Fr	*Week 30*	19 We
20 We	20 Sa	20 Mo	20 Th
21 Th	21 Su	21 Tu	21 Fr
22 Fr	*Week 26*	22 We	22 Sa ◐
23 Sa	22 Mo	23 Th	23 Su
24 Su	23 Tu	24 Fr ◐	*Week 35*
Week 22	24 We ◐	25 Sa	24 Mo
25 Mo ◐	25 Th	26 Su	25 Tu
26 Tu	26 Fr	*Week 31*	26 We
27 We	27 Sa	27 Mo	27 Th
28 Th	28 Su	28 Tu	28 Fr
29 Fr	*Week 27*	29 We	29 Sa ○
30 Sa	29 Mo	30 Th	30 Su
31 Su	30 Tu	31 Fr ○	*Week 36*
			31 Mo

September

1	Tu
2	We
3	Th
4	Fr
5	Sa ☽
6	Su
Week 37	
7	Mo
8	Tu
9	We
10	Th
11	Fr
12	Sa
13	Su ●
Week 38	
14	Mo
15	Tu
16	We
17	Th
18	Fr
19	Sa
20	Su
Week 39	
21	Mo ☾
22	Tu
23	We
24	Th
25	Fr
26	Sa
27	Su
Week 40	
28	Mo ○
29	Tu
30	We

October

1	Th
2	Fr
3	Sa
4	Su ☽
Week 41	
5	Mo
6	Tu
7	We
8	Th
9	Fr
10	Sa
11	Su
Week 42	
12	Mo
13	Tu ●
14	We
15	Th
16	Fr
17	Sa
18	Su
Week 43	
19	Mo
20	Tu ☾
21	We
22	Th
23	Fr
24	Sa
25	Su
Week 44	
26	Mo
27	Tu ○
28	We
29	Th
30	Fr
31	Sa

November

1	Su
Week 45	
2	Mo
3	Tu ☽
4	We
5	Th
6	Fr
7	Sa
8	Su
Week 46	
9	Mo
10	Tu
11	We ●
12	Th
13	Fr
14	Sa
15	Su
Week 47	
16	Mo
17	Tu
18	We
19	Th ☾
20	Fr
21	Sa
22	Su
Week 48	
23	Mo
24	Tu
25	We ○
26	Th
27	Fr
28	Sa
29	Su
Week 49	
30	Mo

December

1	Tu
2	We
3	Th ☽
4	Fr
5	Sa
6	Su
Week 50	
7	Mo
8	Tu
9	We
10	Th
11	Fr ●
12	Sa
13	Su
Week 51	
14	Mo
15	Tu
16	We
17	Th
18	Fr ☾
19	Sa
20	Su
Week 52	
21	Mo
22	Tu
23	We
24	Th
25	Fr ○
26	Sa
27	Su
Week 53	
28	Mo
29	Tu
30	We
31	Th

Notes

Notes

Notes